UNI-VERSES

An Oracle

Verses by David Hadda

Oracle Summary by Peter Rhodes-Dimmer

HERMES-CADUCEUS BOOKS

UNI-VERSES
A HERMES-CADUCEUS BOOK

Hermes-Caduceus Books is an imprint of
Hermes-Caduceus Publishing
Velma Boathouse
Broom Close
Teddington
Middlesex TW11 9RL
ISBN 1 901062 01 5

Printed in the UK by Advanced Design & Marketing

About the Poet

David Hadda's poetry seems inspired by a rather better connection with the Universe than most of us ever achieve. The modern term for his prodigious output might be 'channelling', but his vast collection of poems was started long before this word gained currency. Being a self-effacing man, he would probably never make such a claim!

This kind of work requires great sensitivity and wisdom encompassing a keen observation and understanding of the human condition. David has both in full measure. His creativity expressed itself in his early careers in the areas of music and dance, and he has also worked in broadcasting. He has been a practising healer for the last fifty years.

It was a challenge for such a sensitive man to be born a Jew in Germany in 1923. In the face of an escalating climate of Nazi persecution, he had to emigrate to England at the age of sixteen. Subjected to internment in England, he started writing poetry both as a solace and in order to make himself understood. He discovered the healing powers of the right words at the right time for which his poetry became an effective 'delivery mechanism'.

This book is about parables, organised in the form of an oracle for consultation. David believes that metaphors and analogies are powerful aids to understanding the basic laws which govern all life and if the resolution to some difficulty cannot be easily realised in context, it can often be revealed through the concise insight of an appropriate parable. The poems that form the core of this oracle are taken from the Collected Works of David Hadda and perfectly illustrate these beliefs.

The Poet's Prologue

My poems
Are not finished
until read out aloud
And taken in
To do a real job or two:
Help close a wound –
Disperse an anxious cloud
to shed some warming light
Where things are none too bright,
So you can make your way
out of the messy maze
Of this or that adversity.

Clearly,
It's you
who now completes
What I set out to say –
to bring about.

Without you lending me an ear,
what point is there
In all my writing –
indeed
My being here!

How to use the Oracle

There have always been oracles. The great oracle at Delphi – originally the mouthpiece of the Earth-mother goddess, and later given to Apollo – was one of the best known in ancient history. The Greek heroes often consulted the Delphi oracle in trying times, and when they were being tested in life. There are many other references to oracles including some in the Bible.

So just what is an oracle and how should it be used?

The purpose of consulting an oracle is to assist you on your journey, but not to solve your problems – this is your task alone. The benefit of such guidance is that it gives you another perspective to your current situation. It is a little like the use of radar in World War II. With this new technology, it was possible to tell when there was some enemy aircraft out there, but apart from identifying the general direction it was coming from, the information provided by a single radar station was not very useful. However, people quickly realised that if you took information from two such radar stations some miles apart, you could determine speed, direction, height, and even probable numbers of aircraft. The addition of the input from a second radar system literally provided a different perspective, and by using it intelligently, much additional and vital information could be gathered.

So it is with an oracle. When faced with a situation that you wish to resolve, the oracle provides another viewpoint and through its application you can make further progress. The oracle should *not be used as an absolute*. If you believe what it tells you without applying your own discernment, you simply give your power away to it. This is unlikely either to assist in solving your current issue, or do anything for your personal growth.

You might find the following guidelines helpful. First, try to be very clear about the issue you wish to work with. It may help to write it down concisely since this gives clarity to your thinking. As examples:

The situation is that I keep getting angry with my family, even though I can see that they are not really at fault.

or

I am trying very hard to progress my career, but everything I do just ends in frustration.

or

I do not feel any sense of purpose in my life, and I am depressed about it.

…You get the general idea.

When you wish to use the Oracle, its use is far more effective if you can go somewhere quiet, and meditate on your situation first for a few moments, while you let the day-to-day pressures of life fade into the background. Generally, an oracle will not work too well if there is hassle and noise all around you!

I suggest you then address God, your guides, an Ascended Master – whoever you like to pray to, and ask for appropriate guidance in resolving the situation. Then flip the Oracle open at random, and look at the two pages in front of you. You may want to read the poem first, and see what it means to you. Then look at the oracular summary. Sometimes the poem will have a different significance for you than the summary – it will *resonate* for you – in which case, this is where you should place your attention. At other times, the oracular summary will have an immediate effect, even if the viewpoint being presented seems outrageous, even quite inappropriate. But remember, it is there to give you another point of view – so try to move your thinking to that viewpoint, whatever it may be. By doing this, you stir up the options available for moving forward, and start to get the movement you wanted. Of course, the oracle can also give guidance which is immediately obvious, in which case, so much the better!

There will be occasions when the poem and the oracular summary interact upon your psyche in a very subtle way which is not obvious to your conscious self. You will be aware that something is happening, without understanding the specifics. This too is a valuable experience; the interaction of subtle energies, appearing 'undercover' as it were, below the surface of the words.

At times you may feel like consulting the oracle without a definite situation in mind, simply as a starting-point for a specific meditation. This use can be just as effective as consulting it for a particular reason related to a specific situation. The poems and the oracle can act as powerful aids to a series of meditations and contemplative exercises, and you may find that you are consciously able to extend your perceptions as a result of these.

If, however, you are consulting the oracle for a specific reason I find it very valuable when faced with a trying situation, to ask myself 'What is the lesson here?' This recognises that every difficulty has its lessons to be learned, and if I can identify that lesson early, overcoming the problem – whatever it may be – becomes that much easier.

And having asked for help, be observant of what is happening around you. Listen to 'the whispers'. Having asked for guidance, life will give you a series of hints as to how to move forward – but only if you are alert and sensitive to what you are being guided to do! Otherwise, valuable input will simply pass you by!

The golden rule is: *arrive at a point of clarity about the situation you wish to resolve, and then ask the spiritual world for help in the clearest request you can devise.* You may not always immediately like the new direction that is suggested, but guidance will come, and if you let it, it will move things forward for you. That forward movement, that growth as we overcome each situation, is exactly why we are here on Earth.

It is worth keeping in mind that experience drawn from the ability to resolve and progress life's problems as they arise is how human beings grow in stature, and what moves us along in our human journey of discovery!

Relax: even if your situation does not appear to nourish you now, what you are doing is purposeful. Let your actions unfold harmoniously.

We do need
Warmth and light
To be at home in life:
With warmth
               we can ignite
Some brightness –
With light
We can move out of some distress
    and onward to progress,
Thereby creating Form
                    and Time
    in wretched formlessness.

And even
             if that gives birth
To grinding strife,
We have a hand
             in the unfolding
Of the incomparable flower of Life.

Your situation is undergoing change. It may cause you temporary discomfort but you are working through the problem into a new solution.

I danced through yesterday –
Today
        puts on a hell for me
        I am not sure
                    I can survive......
Why does it sometimes
                    have to be
Such agony to be alive?

Why should new insights
Be distressing
        when they are but a blessing?
Why should some change
Derange us with anxiety,
                    deep fear,
When it was Change
        that brought us here!?

Lighten up and go with the flow. Seeing your situation as heavy going brings your growth to a halt.

I do not want
To suffer any more!
I do not want
To put the blame for it
                    at my own door!

          If only there would be
A way to quit!
But there is none
          ever since
                    this endless
Onward-upward struggle
Was begun.
          And yet
That was for fun!

I want more sunny-funny life,
          not just
Another
          and another one!

Contemplate that your purpose here is to be in harmony as the integration point between Heaven and Earth, and to extend that energy so that it covers an ever-greater area...

My arms reach up and out
       Into the sky –
My legs
Reach down into the soil,
While left and right
                   and roundabout
        there flows the give and take
Of love,
          both into me and out.
Without the full
                  unhindered flow,
        that to-and-fro from sky and ground
                       and fellow-man,
The cloth
        – the sail of me –
Hangs all awry
        and fails to be the undistorting
                       living screen
        on which this life projects its scene.
For I am not a tapestry of things gone by:
        my arms
Reach up to bring the thriving cosmos
        right down into my core,
        that smallish patch of life –
        my legs
Reach down into the soil
To draw life's wholesomeness
        into my body's store,
So I can be
 A fully loving, active member
 Of the community of Man,
And give and take
                  all love I can.

18

Do not be bound by past experience: it was merely that which allowed you to grow to where you are now.

No longer
Is the past my own –
    my sighs,
        groans,
            pains
                and (yes)
    some of my happinesses
Have passed me by –
    their shattering phantom finality
Had no duration
    bears no relation to this,
My present state of being:
    all that I strained to see
Had only transient validity!

Thank God for that!

What I then saw
            could well have done
With more frolicking fun,
            sun-brightness
To turn my arduous escape-advance
    into the laughing lightness
Of a clowning dance!

Ask yourself if this is the time to state your position clearly? If a situation is unjust the remedy for it may lie in your own hands...

I often had to hold my tongue,
Beat down my thoughts
          and stay my hand
In face of deeds that by themselves
Should have cried up to heaven.

I was the suffered guest
Who had no right to see,
          to hear,
             to feel,
To know the doings of his host
And call him to account:
I owed him thanks
For throwing me the chewed-off bone –
     and if he spared me none,
Did he not suffer me
To crouch inside his gate?
     At least
He left me with my life!

Too often have I held my tongue!
     But now that I've come home
I shall no longer silent be
Where I may speak.
I'll throw my voice into the fight
For all
     that weak as it may be
     is still
Fair,
   true
     and right!

Look at your situation against a larger timescale – nothing in the physical world is permanent, yet universal wisdom will always endure.

At last
The sun dried out the ground
    but when the rains
Do fall again,
    the earth will not retain
The shape of what is past...

What happens to the footprints,
    horses' hooves,
        the tracks of carts,
    which sun-dried earth preserved
When autumn rain smooth out her brow,
    wrinkled
    with previous winter's stains –
Those signatures of travellers at the Inn,
Do they just disappear?

Or does a trace endure,
    the atmosphere
        retain their essences
For untold futures to revere?

The scene around you may be more complex than you imagine: simply play your part and all the other elements will come together to form the overall picture.

Fate
Is the sum
        of all that went before,
The sound of all the instruments
Playing at once
        each his own tune.

Whatever writes the score
        must orchestrate the music
In the players' terms –
      in phrases,
            melodies
      their hands,
         their fingers,
             lips and lungs
      can execute.

So do not fear
        nor fight your fate
But prize
       and play your flute
As best you can.

Why over-stretch your resources? Relax the pressure and concentrate on making the best use of what you have. You will then have no need to blame others.

Do play your flute!
But wisely allocate
   your breath,
       strength,
         time,
To make the most sublime
   of all the stirring,
       soaring
Sounds of Man,
   and you will have no need
   to curse
The Master Composer
Of the Universe...

Let enchantment enter your life – if you will allow it, and the sombreness and everyday trivia of your material world will be transformed to a higher plane.

Poems speak to me
    as with a child:

They tell me
How things need to be
And what I used to know
    long,
        long ago –

And while I'm playing by the door,
    they take me by the hand
Into the soul,
Until my spellbound ears
                can hear
Its own, intrinsic music
Flowing
    from the inmost core.

It is time for you to live in the present and not dwell in the past. Only then can the future flow unhindered...

The Here-And-Now
Be given pride of place
    so that the past
Holds its own space
And does not leak
          into the present day:

    Then only
          can the future
    advance
Into the fullness of Life's chance.

    The Present
Is not
The Past's home-territory!

Arrange to spend some time away from the daily clamour and bustle. Contemplate the majesty and tranquillity of nature and your soul will recover its balance.

Driver,
Hold on!
And let those mountains have their say!
How can one hear their sombre silence
Amid the motor's roaring?

Once – only once
I want to listen to that calm
In which the centuries have struck
The balance of tranquillity,
          teaching the struggling hours
To make
                    and hold their peace.

Is this the balm
To ease and heal
          my battle-battered heart?

Perhaps
          here sounds the long sought chord
Resolving in eternal harmony
The warring, clashing sounds
          that until now
Have torn my ears,
                    my thoughts,
                              my mind,
My very soul apart...

By striving for happiness you create your own suffering, and thus you miss the point. Joy is present all around you, just waiting to be let in.

I wish
That someone had told me,
It's not for finding happiness
    that we are here –
             no more
    than for dismembering pain –

But to sustain
Creation's indomitable upward climb
    to something better,
             brighter
Lighter than before:
    because
All life
    finds dark
A bore.

I wish
Someone had told me –
    I would have given
Sweating for happiness a miss
And lapped up all those little joys
        strewn liberally around
And found fulfillment
        – if not bliss.

Resist the temptation to force the pace of your evolving. Your growth arises naturally out of your simply being here.

      Let's raise
The common ground
In little ways –
      instead of rushing,
                    pushing,
      struggling on for ecstasy
      which
         when it comes
      does not seem all that keen
To stay:
      my simply
 Being here
Adds
      to each and every day.

Do not allow yourself to become set in your ways. The danger lies in becoming hard-edged in your thinking. Now is the time to let in more subtle influences...

There is another way
To let intangibles
    imbue the hard and fast reality
With softer,
        kinder
    loving livingness
    to gently
Warm the icecaps of the soul,
    stroking the glaciers into flowing
So they wash off the cutting edges
            of the cliffs,
To form the soil,
      that grows the food
    to flesh the bones of life
        with soothing slopes
        and hugging hills
    of femininity:
It cushioned-cradled you from birth
    and turned into a nurturing paradise
Your very own
        green-smiling earth.

Rise above the details of your situation in order to obtain an overview and thus move into a new perspective.

There is another way
Of seeing,
   of thinking,
      feeling,
        being,
That sees the light in everything
And stays with seeing it:

Just as explorers of the arctic ice
  have their eyes
Fixed on the pole,
  making the endless snows,
  the bitter cold,
    the ruthless storms,
Mere minor details
      on the track
Towards the stirring goal.

  There *is*
Another way…

Problems can teach you a lot about yourself and the way in which you act: are you willing to listen?

I must confess
                    my faith
Is scarred with disasters
                    I cannot easily replace
        with the conviction
That life is on my side.

        What is it
Which upsets
        the oh so fervently imagined
All underlying harmony?

        Surely
The Ultimate
                    must have created
The upset as well!
        Or at the very least
Endowed us with the capability
        at any time
To cook and cock up
All kinds of phantom hell!

Do try to tell me,
                    God
        just
Why –
        oh why!

Don't race against life! Trying to outrun its natural pace only wastes your energy and causes you stress.

My anxious speeding
      drives me right past
Each moment's wholesome peace,
So that it further feeds
      the dirty, deep-down undercurrent
Of sickening anxiety
In which my love of life
              has far too long
    been struggling to survive.

    I run so fast,
I rush right past
             what I've already got –
And then despair
         that what I badly need
I can't find anywhere!

    Stop clowning
And slow down.
    Go
With the flow,
         instead of
For the watershed,
        you silly clot!

Consider that time spent dreaming about the past or speculating about the future is mostly wasted. Concentrate on playing the game that unfolds now.

When
Will You see
It's now for us,
          Lord,
Now!
And not
        Your unperturbed eternity!

    To You
It hardly matters
    that the required,
               necessary
Is,
    was
        or at some future time
Will be,
      as long
As it is part of Your design –
Takes part
        in Your celestial strategy.

But we are at the mercy
Of 'When' and 'How',
Of coming,
        going,
    arriving-staying in the now,
Or leaving
        all bereft –
    something
That You can never be.

Forgive yourself for whatever past mistakes still concern you. Start over! A higher plan allows – has room for – many such experiments!

We have to swim in time and place –
    the flood
    of non-stop changing life
That You have dropped us in –
Where we are bound to sin
By being other than the flow;
    too slow,
        too fast,
            too far ahead –

    And be it
That the purpose of Your handiwork
Will always be beyond our grasp,
Are You prepared
    to let the gory errors
        of Your off-springs' probing
Rob You
    of all
That Your primordial labour pains
Have earned Your caring core?

    Can You
Be so oblivious of our pain
        – if You don't suffer too –
 Or do You simply itch
To start it all from scratch again?

    Would that not be
A little too inane
    as well as
        – do forgive me, Lord –
Celestially insane!

Agonising limits you. If instead you embrace the higher forces that are at work here, your progress will be better managed and lead to a more positive outcome within the larger picture.

God,
  surely You must know
That we need all the help
  You can bestow on anyone.
  You obviously
Are through
With scrutinizing us in detail
                    at arm's length.

  Now that You want us
To wholly step back into You,
Don't try our finite strength
                    to cracking point.
Anoint us with your lenient love
  so we can enter
Erect and tall
        – not crawling on all fours –
Back home into Your caring core.

I want Your guidance,
                    help
In everything I try to do
Since only You can tell
  whether or not
It's in life's plan,
  and though Your know-how
  may have limits too,
Our human sight,
                    perception
Is so slight,
  I do not know enough
Of what I need to know
For my endeavours – however clever,
To fit in with the larger Whole.

Remember: challenging 'what is' – the overall plan – may well be counter productive!

The Cosmic Grand Design
    I do not for the life of me
Want to disturb,
                oppose-malign
With any deed
          or aim of mine:

    there is enough
 Life must get done
Without my littering its run –
I have a vested interest
    to see Creation
Do its best!

Taking a risk when it confronts you will probably expand who you are: while a lack of all risk in your life reduces you. Examine the bottom line – sometimes you must take a chance.

There's no denying
Life
     is an act
 Of faith –
You either trust
              and dare to try
Or start to die.
No use sighing,
          crying.

No use sighing:
           at worst
You die –
     not even that for long –
You'll soon be singing
    another
          and another verse
Of your specific song!

You are now at the leading edge: everything you think or do in consciousness creates its own reality and adds to the cosmic plan...

Say what you will –
Your words
               are spilling over
     into a scene
Where few have ever been before:

Your thoughts are coins
      dropped in the slot
Of God's machine
               for the supply
 Of ever more of living-time –
      until the swelling stream
Carries the device as well
Into its own dissolving in the cosmic sea;
      the end
            and re-beginning
Of the employ of you and me.

      So
         until then
Just be
      and have your song
Add to the ever rising,
              growing
Flow of time
        that carries all along
     into life's endless,
Boundless Destiny.

Take the opportunity to acknowledge something joyous and spontaneous! Break the mould of daily habit and celebrate life!

Not just the young,
We too
Do need a chance
          with all our grand advancing
For dancing,
       fooling,
             romping,
                  prancing –
  simply
Exuberancing:

Life is there
Not just to live
But for enhancing!

Frequently take time to be quietly with yourself. Retreat into your inner space and your world will expand in the stillness.

How precious
                is this stillness
Once silence is imposed!

    With doors
                    closed
To the outside clamour
                    of our frantic strife,
        here
            lies
        all that I need
To feed my life:
        fear and pain
Have lost their sting
                        and everything
Begins to sing...

    How blissful
Is this stillness!

When confronted and constrained by inflexibility, remember that infinity has room for many viewpoints!

Each one
Is groping differently
For what there is to grasp,
                    to reach
        right here inside
Or way beyond our common sphere.

No wonder
            each one
Is finding something else
That others cannot see
                        and asks
'How can that be?'

Do not despair:
        thank God
For life's unflustered versatility
        we are so privileged to share!

Each one is groping differently
        for what there is to grasp,
To reach in here,
                out there
        beyond our common sphere,
No wonder
            that we all
Keep finding something else!

Thank God
            for His own versatility
We could not be more privileged to share.

For now, let yourself be in the fog of confusion – do not fight it. It has a purpose: the salient point can then emerge with clarity, unencumbered by its surroundings!

We do not really
See much more
    than what the fog
    leaves unconcealed –
Indeed
      even our field of vision
    reveals so much
That our awareness will not touch.

The fog does justice
To each tree
      all on its own,
Leaves out
      and hides away
What is outside my Now
    which I don't really need to see.

And, strange:
    there in the mist
The mystery around one tree
Is greater
      than the forest's spell!
Then we as well have merit,
        meaning,
          splendour
    Each on his own
And not
    as part of human kind alone!

Are you sure that you are seeing what really matters? Or have you missed the point!

It seems
We cannot see
   the tree
For all the wood,
   the wide,
     wide open
scenery!

Talk to those outside your immediate circle, welcome fresh viewpoints and thus you will find a new angle on your situation!

Each blade of grass
Adds its own drop of dew
     to wash
The passing traveller's feet
Just
     as our desert-fathers
Used to do
For strangers
          passing through.

What gladdening event
     to have the new
Enter
     our so familiar tent!

Militant fundamentalism in any walk of life points to a dangerous polarity. There is no such thing as 'only one way' in our creative Universe!

Are we again
In the marketplace
    where different faiths
Outbid each other
        for the monopoly
On the Divinity?

Don't bother!
Your zeal and zest
Won't make
    the Father-Of-All-There-Is
Love you more
        than the blessed
    lesser rest!

If you really want to be miserable you have that right: but remember you also have another choice!

       Some right now
Are laughing
    and some
             right now
Are crying –
    some
         now
Are being born
            and some are dying...

Life
    housing both
    seems to show
No preference.
    so
       we are free
To choose
        whichever it will be...

And I know
What I want for me!

Whatever troubles you now, let laughter into your life. Your current situation and all its tribulations will then fall into proper perspective!

Resist despair:
     it does not get us anywhere
But ever deeper
     into those hopeless swamps
Of helplessness
         than hitherto!

     Let's give ourselves
To fun,
     joke,
        song and dance
     to give the best of life
A laughing-loving chance!

Keeping laughter
In
   is contrary to everything
We are about –
Not letting out
        our fun
Must annoy the Cosmic One.
     Was not
By His laughter
        all begun?

Give yourself to joy and you can rise above the cloying energies which others seek to lay on you!

     I give myself
To joy –
         no matter
               what clogs my sight –
Until life's basic,
             vital brightness
      comes shining through –
      not just for me
But for you too:
      your moans and groans
I just can't take –
            they shake my love of life
To breaking point
          more
Than my unhappinesses do.

You are intimately linked with all that is and everyone there is around you. Try to assimilate the scene from a viewpoint of inter-connectedness.

We don't just
Overlap a little
         here and there –
There is not much
         if anything
We do *not* share.
    We merely stare
From different windows
    on to the selfsame scene:
Each one of us
    a crystal,
         a glittering facet
Of a star-sized,
         Earth-tinted,
 Diamond
    floating in space,
    forever slowly turning
   to show us
All there is to see
    of glowing,
         burning
 Life's eternity.

It is time to focus on the situation in hand, rather than to expend your energy on what was, or speculate on what might be.

Look
     where the book of life
Falls open
        in your hand
    and then
Read on from there:
    it saves you
Wading through
    what is right now
Of little relevance for you.

    Or
Have you living-time
To spare?

Observe the scene around you carefully and allow it to mirror reality back to you...It helps you to know where you are in your life's journey.

Only the land
                    can tell you
How the land lies –
        which way
The wind is blowing –
What's arising
                    on the horizon,
What is receding-fading
        and what comprises
Your lot,
                your task
This very day-of-days.

        Only the land can tell
The lie of the land;
It is the only brand of knowing
Worth going for –
        the rest
                is badly soiled
 With self-deception
                    at the very best.

Move through your present painful moments and let them go...do not get attached to the misery — then all that will be left are the joys of life.

Past joys
        are lodged forever
In all the present moments
                yet to come,
    while pain
Would soon get flushed away
    with every dawning,
                new-born day
    if with our fears
We would not cling to them,
    force them to stay.

What makes us play this gormless game?
    To give our luscious life
A bad, sad name?

Consider what will represent the completion of the process you are now engaged in, and then hold that completion as your focus.

Each sound
                needs turning
Into music,
                all blindness
Into sight:
          not only darkness into light
          and dimness into brightness.
Chilling black-and-whiteness
          does need turning
Into colours' deep delight!

        Clearly
It is for this
                that we are here –
Not
        by day
To fight each other
        and ourselves
                by night!

It will aid you now to let go of your heavier issues – they have served their purpose. Don't lose sight of the fact that you are here to enjoy yourself!

Where is that humorous exuberance
That first gave life a chance –
Which started all
    and ever since
All is about!

Where is the revelling mirth
    with which life scrunched itself
Into a bustling ball
        called Earth!

I've tried
    as hard as anyone
To do my best –
    and if that was not blest
With more success
    and seems not to have done
    all that much good,
At least
 I have not added still more
    to that dreary mess –
Depressing everybody's zest
        for going on.

Mind you,
I think I should have had more fun –
    but then
Does that not go
        for almost everyone?

The world's resources and those of the Cosmos are largely constant, reflecting all possibilities: it is only the images of your mind that determine whether your choices are positive or negative.

It's not
      that God
Is absent from a thing,
But in our choices
    we either listen
To His blazing splendour
                sing full out
Or hear Him slumbering in the wings,
    which he alone can do
Concurrently
          but we can only see
One at a time
    for us to mope
             or gloat about
In praise
    or bitter condemnation
Of the all indispensable Divinity.

    Everything
Is always there
And it is up to us
    what we select
           to take in or reject,
    remembering
To reach up to a higher sphere
    only
When we have learned to be
All here.

The Cosmos is neutral towards you! You are the creator in your physical world. Draw on the cosmic abundance to support your own creativity...

The Lord has not given –
The Lord has not taken –
The name of the Lord is blessed
Because He neither giveth

                        nor taketh
But moveth all

             forever
     onward
To higher realms of His glory.

How could He give
While no one – nothing,
Stands outside of Him
To take,

         receive
If anything were given.

       Nor can the Lord
Be taken from,

       reducing Him to less than all:
How could He take,

     since being all,

                 possessing all –
He has no need of anything.
And even the bereaved
Weeps amid His limitless abundance,

     not knowing
That new wealth is sucked into his soul

     as the departing draws away.

The Lord does not give nor take –
The name of the Lord is blessed
For He moveth all unceasingly
To ever higher realms of His glory.

You have the power to manifest all you need in your physical life. Simply be clear about what you want and then ask!

Don't send your prayers
Out into the blue
Merely on spec –
    in case there's something
       somewhere out in space to hear.

Without you sensing us,
We are ignored, passed by,
Till we ourselves
          can be no longer sure
That we are here, exist!

But anyhow:
Whether you are part of us
    or we of you
Or all of us
Components of a larger whole,
We too
    – like you –
Must sometimes change our mind.
We can't stay blind
     to what till now
Was out of range for Man –
Just as for Spirit-kind.

   So,
Do address your prayers
         without fail
More clearly,
    with a surer hand,
  or they might land up
Getting lost
In the celestial mail!

All possibilities are available. The higher you set your sights, the higher your achievements will be...

I'd like to have climbed
A mountain top –
    not the steepest,
             highest
        proudest of them all,
But just a mountain among mountains –
And know that I don't have to stop,
 I still can climb
             to the heights of my choice,
    and that mountains are there
For all to scale:
          welcoming,
              glorious,
                 joyful,
Not daunting,
        forbidden – forbidding
    and forsaken.

    And neither need one in the end
Fall from on high,
    but can choose
To go on roaming mountain ranges
    even
        – once the wings have grown –
Fly off into space
    or descend in one's own good time
To hug the snug, safe valley floor…

We thus have no more cause to think
    that heights are out of bounds for us,
      forever native only
To the dreary, degrading depth,
Below the mountain's brink.

Be aware of the defences you build around you. Are they perhaps locking out precisely that which you desire to have in your life?

We older ones
Are veritable minefields
                              for anybody else!
        And every mine
We rigged up on our own,
        dug into place laboriously:
        all
To keep everybody out –
        especially the Lurking Enemy
Who threatens change
                              to the precarious way
        we knotted up the day.

And then
                we spend the sleepless nights
Longing,
                yearning
For some human company!

        (The hell?
We older ones
                are mine-fields
To ourselves as well!)

See yourself as part of a greater whole. Embrace it, go with the flow and you will see that you are not alone.

The answer lies
Not with the empty silence
                    behind closed eyes,
But in the open gaze
        at all
That now before them lies:
From right down
                    at our feet
        upward to and outward from
The blazing stillness of our skies –
        not rising,
                    leaping,
                            flying,
        but growing
To embrace with body,
                    mind
                            and heart
The boundless whole
        of which we are not just a part.
Nothing is independent of the whole
        and you can only
Lonely be
When all the rest of you
                    – the vastly larger rest –
You do not see.

A New Age! At last we can leave the doubts and fears of the past behind. Insist on optimism and see it transform every area of your life!

This
     is the turning of the Dark
Into the Light!
Now
     we take flight
Into that vital brightness
     of which the Night
Has always dreamed:
     the Dark will soon be seen
As just an aching memory
          of what has been
     for life to be henceforth
Of any suffering exempt!

Delight
     in your *igniting*
More of Light,
     and soon
The Night will fade away
     until all suffering
 Has died...

The dark is merely the tunnel to lead you to the light: appreciate that it has a purpose – just don't get attached to it!

The dark
Is incubating-room,
                    the womb
        for what will soon
Loom into the light of day
                        to zoom eventually
Into the boundless skies
        of all
Reality
            will ever want to be –
        that always sprouting-blooming
Pleasure-park
                    where we,
        perched at the edge of dark and light
        are meant to be
Gatekeepers,
                    gardeners,
                            midwives
        for what is waiting in the wings
To stride onto the stage
        of a more touchable,
                            embraceable
Love-physicality.

        Alas, our eyes
Must see so much of dark
To ease the struggling babe
        across the tightest border
Into caring Light!

Only by embracing and taking in the new can you grow into it. Thus, by moving on, you can make this a continuous and positive process.

First
 Drink in the new –
Only that
                will quench your thirst.
Then
        you can make your way
            into and through
The present day.
        In the New
There's plenty to look forward to
        as in the past
There's much to leave behind,
                        let go at last,
        that in the present
You can hug
                what has grown close:
        closeness
Occurs
            though you can nurture it,
                        can make it grow –
        alas,
You can't produce-induce it
    nor make it stay.

        Hence hug the huggable
The while you may,
        but then
Move on –
            away...

Spend time regularly in the stillness of your inner space, for stillness is a great healer...

The sun
        is cutting through the haze
Into a blaze of fun
              ever since
Existence was begun!

Sons and daughters of the universe
Stillness
        floats you through all dearth
To the riches of your earth –
              there
Where buds and blossoms pop,
            explode
You were given your abode.

    Suffering
Is not your lot
    unless you make it so:
Go to stillness –
          stillness
Strokes away
      your every woe.
    For
Stillness
        is opening all doors
That should not have been closed
    and helps us
To adore
      the way things are
And asks no more.

110

Our beginning and our end lies in stillness: consider therefore that all activity is merely transition.

    Stillness
Has always been
             and will be
             time and time again
    both
The beginning
             and the end of everything
But not the in-between:
    for one thing
    there is also
Bliss
    when all creation is a-singing
    ringing the bells
Of giving birth
             into the lap of earth
    and Universe.

It's then
        the In-Between
    is clearly seen
To be all up to Man.

By putting energy into hopes and fears you bring them into reality. Be pragmatic: stick with the hopes!

Fears
      have a way
Of generating
What was not going to appear,
      but then
Our joyful hoping
              may steer
Many a pleasure into the real day
      when otherwise
It would have passed us by,
         eloping to some other sphere.
     and it's our dreams
Coming to life
       that keep us coping
            while we are here.

     When life
Is none too nice
          or just a bore
    we want to know
What it is all about!
    Yet
      when it's just
One pleasure after another,
    we do not bother
To ask:
     what for?
But relish it
And go for more!

Forget where you started in life – it will only hold you back. Instead, focus on who you are becoming.

The Past?
Erase –
    and leave no trace
    that might debase
Your present place in time –
        that timeless space.
    The climber,
        summit-bound,
Must be committed
To the ground under his feet:
    his base-camp,
        starting point
Is now irrelevant –
        since obsolete.
And don't forget,
    the summit that you'll reach
Is not the end
        to your ascent's eternal climb
    to the Sublime
With which we all eventually must blend.
Man's seeming separation of The Fall
    cannot for long
Appear to contradict-oppose
Life's cosmic Oneness –
    that ever-unfolding,
        festive
Heaven and earthly Choral song.

Try to see your life as the progression of a dance – then ask yourself: is yours a waltz or a tango?

No longer is the past
My own.
    I move,
        I modulate
        from one tonality
    into another
And yet another key!

    Praise be
The symphony is without end:
I rise,
    descend
        and rise time and again
Into another and yet another
Turn of phrase,
        of tune,
           song,
        choral mass.

My sap flows in and out
    of different branches of life's tree,
Grows into flowering
    until the blossoms wither,
           drop
And join the soil
        to feed,
          give birth
To yet another sprout
        singing its way
    out into
An all new cadence
In the ever revelling forest-symphony.

It is important to value age and the experience that comes with it and see it as part of a continuous process...consider who else might then contribute to your life.

Do not
Take ageing
All for granted –
We need to earn
The privilege of having learned
That there's no end to anything:
    we just extend
             from this one patch
   to yet another
         on our infinite itinerary!

No need to worry –
         do not bother!
Just let life be
       with moderate impunity:
   what is there
       you can know
With any certainty
But that Life will adhere
To its incorrigible continuity!
   Yes,
Ageing is no mean reward
For having been through thick and thin,
Without despairing,
         giving in
   or getting bored!

Thank God
      I can afford
   to sport
A more and more embracing
   smile type
Grin!

The child in you has a lighter perspective on life: let it out – give expression to your sense of fun!

I can afford
        to sport
An all-embracing grin!

When all is said and done,
We are a bunch of kids
     pretending to be dad or mum –
Oh God
      – what fun!
    And grown-ups
There are none...

We spend so much of our time and energy 'second guessing' life! This game is not a useful one – we miss out on so much fun!

Surprise, surprise:
    most of our fears
Do not materialize –
        they were not real
    from the start!

    The rest
We had a hand in cooking,
        tarting up
    ourselves,
When it is in our interest
    to manifest
        and savour
Each bit of pleasure arrived at
        and created
    by the living day,
Indulge and revel
    in the caring peace of night!

Why not join in
    with all the good times.
Life, is having
        the very fun
    for which existence was created
By the Eternal One!

Even if the situation appears hopeless, and especially in an emergency, you cannot afford an inner collapse. Use all the support that is around you...

There is no time
                    – no room –
For rank despair!

    It is precisely there
Where it wells up
                    that we can't spare –
    must swear allegiance to –
The life we share
With all there is,
                    with all we are
In its unfolding splendour
                    flowering everywhere!

    There only
Seems
A need for dark despair
When we don't see,
                    are not aware
Of all your helpers there
    inside and next to us
As way out there.

Remember that in the peaceful moments of your inner space, guidance from higher realms is always available to you...

'Where will You speak to me?'

Wherever there is peace
There is my shrine –
I am all peace,
               all peace is mine.
So
   go for peace
In everything you do,
    And I,
In everything
         will speak to you.

If you really want to be happy, you must make a commitment to it. You have to work at happiness and will it into your life.

Man is not born
With happiness within his heart,
    nor is it in his tool-kit
    from the start:
    he must create
And grow it there
    until it spreads
        and branches out
Into the world
        right here and everywhere
    – even begins to sing
        and sound all-round -
    so it not just resembles
But becomes
    the living smile,
        then laughter
Of all life's Joy-Divinity
        for ever after.

The will
    to fun and laughter
That is the vital thing –
    the landing-strip
For lilting lightness to wing in
    so we no longer
Merely mutter,
    talk
But hum and sing –
    no longer crouch,
        stand,
        walk,
    but find ourselves advancing
Lightly dancing!

The need to rush through life is a human frailty. Take a leaf from nature's book – everything in its own good time...

Says the park:
'Don't rush with me!
You only rush
When there is not enough to see!
But here
with all my greenery
There is so much to draw your sight
And touch your mind
and soul,
You might as well
Slow down,
hold on
To still your thirst for all the thrills
life will distil.

Walk leisurely
until
You've had your fill...'

There is a season for all things: sometimes you must simply wait while the natural cycles unfold. Nature brings about its own change.

Shedding their leaves
 The trees
         lay wreaths of grief
For summer
       now deceased,
The while their blazing colours
   already
Wave their welcome to the sun,
   however far away
        beyond the grey horizons.

     From now on
Trees and all
        must live unwaveringly
For Spring
      bound to wing in one day,
   no matter
What chillingly unfeeling things
 Frozen-hearted snow and ice
   are sure to say.

Every individual has a different vision of the future and each has a right to choose: you cannot mandate how it will be for others.

Don't tell the future
What to bring:
      it's got to sing its song
To multitudes of ears,
                           each
      clamouring to hear
A different melody.

    And though
                tomorrow
Has a thousand voices,
      in simply doing its own thing
It gives us all the choices
      for doing
Our own thing.

    Let all bells ring!

Remember life is made up of new beginnings: there is always room for another. After all, it was change which brought existence into being!

A world of light
                    emerging from the dark,
Igniting every blade of grass,
                              heart,
                                    mind
Under the flaming dome of sky.

A world of light –
                    and yet
It's just a spark of the all-filling flame
        that heats the cosmic temperature
To living-point
                    to lift existence
            out of staying
                        endless eternities
Tediously the same –
                    the same –
                              the same...

Let's start afresh,
                    afresh,
                              AFRESH!
Not stay enmeshed
In what might have been right before –
        not try
To take it through into the rising day
        without the certainty
It still does justice to the New!
        There won't be any room
For the no-longer-true:
The Truth
            will now be much,
                        much more!

*Only by being all that you can be −
expressing all − is your life's goal
progressed to its fullest...*

The time for humbleness
Is passed –
     we can't afford
Our customary stumbling,
    our gambling,
          shambling,
             reeling
   anymore.
Next time we fall
A final blast
       might rob us of all chance
To learn,
    advance by crawling,
  let alone
By walking tall!

   If we don't use
Our widest stride
   there will be nothing left
To be worth going for –
   nothing more
To even lay our bungling at its door:
All will be shattered
   by death's
Final roar.

The joys of life, its regular pleasures are the building blocks from which you can construct your own bliss...

Every bit of pleasure
You give yourself
            lifts a king-sized joy
Straight from life's bulging treasure shelf
            onto the vacant tray
Of your waiting day.

Life
Wisely takes its cue
            from what we choose
To go for,
                    acknowledge –
            just as
From what we simply will not do.

The past?
                    The present?
I say goodbye to all of this:
I must make room
For more of bliss!

Keep any pressure on you to hurry strictly temporary. You are greatly diminished if it becomes your normal mode of operation.

If you must hurry
Scurry not too long –
    don't let your peace
Go for a song!

 If rush you must
          let it be just
    to get you
To a less stressful stretch
          further along,
  – though
Peace postponed,
      foregone
          time and again
Might keep it out of sight and reach
Until the end
     much later on...

    Who
        will go on dropping in
    on someone
Who is always rushing out
    and cannot even stop
To say 'hello'?

Doubts and interpersonal issues are the anchors that hold us back from growth and progress. Let your purpose be the shining star that draws you ever forward...

There must not be
One bitterness
                    that holds you back,
One dark spot
                    that impairs your shining
        when shining
Is the purpose,
                function,
                        task
        of every life,
And any falling short of it
        The only cloud on radiant horizons,
Ablaze with ever greater joy
        for one and all.

        Oh,
Not a doubt
Must cloud the rising Day of Days,
        to raise us
                    out of all dreary,
                    weary yester-greys!
And it is every star's to shine
        and not to hide behind
But melt
        – and drain right off –
        all age-old
Interstellar grime.

Be sure you do not give ageing a bad name! Use it as a learning process to lead you to the rich fullness your life can assume...

That I am growing older
Is fine by me,
As long as ageing
                    is not defined
        as the decline
Into relentless atrophy,
But an advancing
        to getting more things right
So I can make my entrance
    from the wings of wimping impotence
Onto the centre-stage of life
        with its enlivening
Bright floodlight!

Trying too hard in life means that you will miss much of value in your surroundings – ultimately, this is not a rewarding exercise.

Don't choose
So hard a path,
You have to keep your eyes
Glued to the ground you tread:
      you'll miss
            and lose
The beauty of the scenery
            that you traverse!
      and it's our duty
To enjoy all bliss
The earth surrounds us with.
      So go
      and choose
The more rewarding path instead.

We are in an era of accelerating change – a positive process. Don't let your need for stability blind you to the possibilities of change...

Do not blame change
That it curtails
　　　　　our modicum of happiness
Before it's getting stale!
Don't rail against the very thing
That brings an end
　　　　　　to endless suffering.

　　As long
As there is change
There's hope.
　　Life
Is but boundless scope,
　　and hope
Is never out of place:
It faces upwards
　　　　　and not down,
　　hence
Frowns are out of place
　　　　　　on your –
　　and Life's – exuberantly smiling
Clowning face.

　　As long
As there is change
There's hope!

Only if you recognise that there are many valid paths, can you learn from others and thus strengthen your own path.

    May this
Not be
Another marketplace
For peddling one's own brand of faith,
    but that
          rare
Dedicated space
          for each
To reach out
       or reach in
    for his uniquely precious glimpse
Of Life-Divine,
        the richer, nearer
    to that illusive whole
    by
      your God
Looking different
        from mine.

All processes in life have a natural sequence. Measuring them or imposing a structure on them won't give you control over them...

155

Don't let yourself
Be run by clocks –
                    it only blocks
The pulse of living universes
                    knocking at your door.
You cannot lock life out,
                    tell fate
        it's come too early
                    or too late,
And shut your gate to it
                    – or drag it in –
        because the clockhands
Do not correlate!

        However long you have to wait,
The sun
        – as fate –
Does always rise on time:
Open your ears
                    to the gait of life
And you will hear
Each living moment chime!

Be still! Contrary to your belief, your total stillness fulfils a high creative purpose.

Don't ever think
You're doing nothing:
We're never
              doing nothing!

    And even
When we fail to do
        what we set out
        to bring about –
And even
            when it seems
We're being idle –
                doing nothing,
We are still doing
God's creative will
        nothing can ever
    Help fulfil.

If you need help, STOP: only then will you stay still long enough to receive it...

Happiness
Is not a leisure time pursuit
To be indulged in
               after work
      or basked in on vacation.

It is the vital,
             never-ending task
Of climbing out
             of the vast irksome murk
                obstructs our way
Into another
        worth-living day.

Insights – when followed – are your way forward. Trust them!

Insights
Are matches
        struck in the dark
   for us to ignite
Warming fires
       in the chill of night.

Insights
    are matches
         struck in the dark
To give us bearings
   once we embark on the trek
To the Land of Light.

You have a duty to nurture your thoughts and to follow them through to realisation...

Thoughts,
        even deeds
  – just as seeds –
Are only vessels
    for life to fill
    according to *its* needs.

We
Do the sowing,
        planting –
And all of life
The growing.

Prayer is a two-way communion: it does not fulfil its potential if you are too busy to hear the answers!

Don't pray so much
But listen
     and let occurrences
     relay life's answers to your pleas.

Question
        and answer,
Request
        and satisfaction of your need,
They may be different things for you,
But they are one
     in the inter-galactic diocese.

Don't overpray:
     the day
Is more important
        than your aspirations –
The living moment
Has the right of way.

There are many options available to you. Focus on as many of them as are indeed possible before you make your choices...

Between
What is to come
            and what can never be,
There lies a no man's land
        of what could possibly
            – although not necessarily –
        be coaxed by us
Into too-dense-for-words existence
                    on our earth:
An *all*-man's land,
                quite large enough
To keep us busy
For something like eternity.

You are part of a far larger system than you realise: play your part and the universe will play its own role...

     I know
No drop of water
Flows alone,
But
     – like all pebbles on the beach –
Each has a past and present
                    of its own
To teach its wave
How far to reach –
What other places it could go,
    but also
    what fulfilment grows
In ponds of stillness
    where water
Rests
    and its incessant flow foregoes...

If you go with the flow you cannot be stopped on your journey – only delayed a little from time to time as you choose to linger...

If we are sailing
With the stream,
                    the winds and waves
Can but divert us
For a time.
        Though it may often seem
Like an eternity,
                    inexorably
The waters bear us to the sea,
        and what we love
Is rations,
            boat and rudder
        on our voyage to the port
Of our distinctive destiny.

I am a wave,
Am free to flow
                far and wide
Within the ocean's ebb and tide.

*Co-operation leads to community.
Ask yourself: are you listening to
others, are you truly sharing?*

175

Where you
Can come to me
                and I to you
        to help
To bring into reality
        what you can see
                        need be –

        where you
Can have me share
        in carrying a stone
                that you want to take home –

Where I can add
                what I have grown
To everybody's meal,
                not just my own –

        where everybody
 Tries to know
        when it is time
To keep each other company
        and when you
                        for a while
        need to be left alone –

That
Is Community
                for me.

Your path may be narrow and difficult – but if you share your experience, the path becomes so much easier.

For us on earth
The path
        is necessarily
A narrow one:
           it has to run
Between debarring individualities,
           excluding territories
               on every side,
    and only
Where they overlap
          to coincide
          in some small way
    with us,
To stitch together
           disparate existences
Into a loving living-whole.

    Perhaps
That here alone
          in all the universe
We can look over fences,
           garden walls
    to catch a glimpse of inner worlds
So alien to our own,
We need a loving fellow-soul
To urge us on
          and to console.

The past was framed to be exclusive and excluding – only now are we becoming inclusive...

Everything
Will now be blended:
the New
With what has ended –
the fresh, bold, Young
With the so wise and gentle-old,
until all differences
Embrace
and hold each other dear
so that the so-called dead
Blesses
and nurtures
The newly-wed Today.

No more cessation
but ever upward
Transformation!

We must move on
from 'either/or'
to
'This-as-well-as-that'
Under a new type common hat
that can be worn
By several heads at once,
living their own lives
Unimpaired
while gladly joining in
The newest Common Dance.

Take time for reflection and listen to your innermost voice. Day-to-day irritations will then be soothed away as the larger picture takes hold of you.

Thank God,
              this is a place
For stillness
              and not
For spilling last week's beans –
       For listening to
some out-of-town transmission
But tuning in
                     each
To his own internal singing
Well beyond all daytime sound,
       exploring
Our cosmic inner sanity
We've been too long ignoring.

You must decide the path your journey takes. Any other decision will lack the appropriateness your own choice confers.

Sooner
              or later
One comes upon a path –
       and though
It speeds one's travelling on,
       it is the way
That others went
              to their own destinations
Not likely to be yours
              or mine.

And so
      – sooner or later –
      it's
wading through the thicket
             once again,
To cut a path
          – one's own –
Through more of life's
           unmapped terrain.

Much of one's travelling
Has to be done alone...

Your journey is more important than your destination. For it is your experiences which shape you and determine what you will be when you finally arrive.

Surely
The path I take
Is as important
                    – if not more so –
        than my destination:

What happens to me
                    on the way
        not just determines
        when and in what shape
I will arrive
                    – and leave.
If I should fall
                    and break a leg –
I won't be getting there
At all!

Anxiety acts like a millstone around your neck to weigh you down and keep you from progress.

Why do you plant
Anxiety into your world
When it is not a tree
                    to give you shade or fruit?
It is a weed
That feeds on you
                    and drags you down
When you are stretching-reaching up
        trying,
Longing to succeed!

        Anxiety
Is never in our interest –
        indeed
It does foil every quest
                    on which you set your heart
        by draining you
Of all the fervour
        with which life blessed your soul.

        Don't let anxiety
Control the purpose of your life
Or it will sabotage
                    and stall
Each struggling step you take
Towards your whole life's goal!

Is the opportunity in front of you so large you simply cannot see it?

I threw so large a piece of bread
                              into the pond,
The ducks ignored it,
          where they had fed
                    on smallish crumbs before –
          until
                    a little gang of three or four
Began to break it down
                              to share...

Abundant blessing
                              can be more
Than light-starved lives can bear:
          we can't believe our luck
Until our reaching for
                              and touching it
          bears witness
 That it's there
And takes us through the doubts
          "It's all too good
                    to really be true."

     Perhaps
                    our aches and pains
 Need to arise
To make believable
                    our greatest blessings
To our too startled,
                    joy-dazed eyes.

Thoughts are a vital part of the creative process – they are a powerful tool which we find all to easy to ignore. If you want to create, listen to yourself!

A thought
Is the beginning
Of some new thing,
                    a deed –
The lifting of the hammer
        to forge a shape
That needs to be –
        the world must come to see;
        the thought
Flows into sound –
                        its structured air
Grows into deed,
                the deed,
                        an act
Bestows another factor
                        upon reality
To join into relating.

        A thought
Needs voicing - stating,
                        acting on.

        To think a thought
Is the first stirring
Of a real thing.

We are entering a period of transformation – go with it! Don't hang back in the same old routines.

Has winter
Ended for you too?

Has your wild courage
                        seen you through
The choking sameness of your past
Into some vast,
                  new realms
        of sweeter,
 Richer fruit
                and scope?
        Did you indeed
Elope into a fuller
Present day?

    If so
Do let us know:
        perhaps we too
Ought to pack up
                    and go...

    If not –
            I fear
We'd better stay
        here
                where your restless striving
Has made you rear
                and swerve away from us
To get away –
                away...

You are but a microcosm of the Universe. Remember that, see the larger picture and life will be more harmonious...

I can't speak
For the universe,
But if we devastate this earth
It couldn't stay the same.
Without a function,
role to play
within the feasting whole,
Neither the earth
nor we
Would be around,
so that
With one part missing
or conked out
That whole
is bound to be
Less sound
and that would be
– to say the least –
A shame!

You may feel that the struggle is not yet over – but the breakthrough is in sight! Don't despair!

The grass
Is white
       with frozen dew –
So is my hair
       from all the overbearing years...

Another Spring is overdue:
       grass
May look fresher in freezing frost,
But my own freshness
Soon gets lost
       in splintering cold...

       Why does not winter
Pack it in,
       give up,
    grow old
And die!

As you move forward on your journey, remember – being first off the mark does not ensure arrival at the next destination! Premature haste can be an obstacle to your growth...

For weeks
One of my apple trees
Has kept his firm,
                    taut,
                            red-green buds
Steadfastly shut
While all the other ones have
        with the first shy trial run of sun
Rushed headlong
        into full, white blooming.
        Now
That the summer-warmth
        has come to stay,
                            is looming large –
        they have already lost
Their bright,
                light bridal dress
        to
            oh, so-cruel,
                            innocently unexpected
Frosts.

        But that one prim
Strict apple tree
        has suddenly
Abandoned all reserve,
        has flung his buds
Wide open to the heat...

        Guess
Who it was
                that grew last fall
        the finest
Richest fruit of all!

While failure can be a step forward on your ultimate journey, doubt brings everything to a halt and holds up progress...

Failing
Is for us too
A possibility –
      although for us
It's just a stepping stone
      to the eventual achieving –
The while with you
It's halting
        your striding out,
    your walking on
Till you succeed.

We need your loyalty,
        your trust
That we can exist,
    so that we can persist
In doing all we can
To help you onwards,
        up.
Your doubting
Partly cancels your request to us
    and leaves less room
    for us
To do our best.

Invest us
With your trust
        or you must walk
Alone,
    prone,
To each whim of wind...

Optimism sheds its own light in the face of problems, so that it is easier to see the possible solutions...

Earth
      is not
The opposite of Heaven –
    the sticky clay,
        the soggy bog under our feet
    that holds us captive to the ground:
It sprouts
      and grows us
    up towards the sky
Till we are heaven-bound –
That all life-loving launching pad
    for rising as high
        into the ever-animating,
        resuscitating sun
    as anyone
Would ever wish to fly.

    Oh,
      I will always
    stand by
This loveliest of stars:
I owe it everything so far!

    No matter
What the cleverest of cynics say,
      the moaning sad-sacks groan,
 I'll love this earth
Until my dying day.

You may not know it when you stand in the midst of magic – only later does awareness overtake you!

The charm,
                the sheer enchantment
Of where I've been
      I had not seen
While I was there!

      Only
In looking back
      the magic of the scene
Catches my senses,
      walks through to,
                takes by surprise
My eyes,
      my ears
      and they begin to hear
The so bewitching chant
                steering me
      back
Into the heart of life –
With which my searching consciousness
      always
Merely interferes.

Don't always look to the far horizon to realise your aims and ultimate goal. The building material is to hand and the place is right here!

Out in the dark
      below the luminous evening sky,
   there I am free
To build me my Jerusalem.

   Why must I wait
Until I drive right through her streets?
   I need no rocks
              under my feet
To authorize my dreams:
Some shades of dark
         and moonbeam streaks
Seem just as much
Jerusalem!

Inspiration is often to be found in some new and fresh detail: so don't overlook it or seek to rise above it...

It is the new –
Some freshly folded phrase
    for which my ear,
My tongue is waiting –
A different tune
           in a quite different mode
    to curl itself around
And up a different scale,
    then
Flutter down
       and come to rest
    in this old,
Yearning heart of mine,
           imparting it
    an unforeseen
      – hence so unsettling –
Rejuvenating glow.

What bliss
      whenever
 It is so!

Counsel from others is helpful, but be true to yourself rather than have others direct you.

Don't let the others
    tell you
What to do –
    but listen to
What *they* can see –

    And let their view
Add depth
        to your decision
To go
    – no matter what they say –
Straight out
For your own vision,
        unbothered
    by approval –
Or derision!

Even though you may take the right action at every point of your journey, you may rarely see the results of your decisions...

Rarely
      can we stay
      to see the seeds we planted
Root
      and bear fruit...

      We are not farmers
But nomads
         en route into eternity:

      And yet
Whatever we say
Flows out into life's universe
      where it is bound to change
The melody it sings,
         the very ashram-hall
In which we'll come to live thereafter:

Oh, it is us
Who change the flavour
         of the cosmic brew
      into more groaning woe
Or lightly loving laughter!

If your journey appears to be a steep climb, keep looking ever onwards and upwards!

On my climb
Up the incline
To more of brighter joy
                        – if not bliss –
    I do not want to waste my time
Looking down
            into the dim abyss of my past:
    thank heaven
It did not last!

Even here,
                even now,
 It's all too often
                    grey enough
        as it is!

If you keep moving the goalposts in your life's 'game', how can you expect to score?

Don't go
For something more
           until you've made the most
Of what you have right here and now!
    Why try
To somehow reach,
                fly up into the sky –
      strain to 'attain a higher sphere'?
You can't obtain
      what life
Has not yet delivered to your door!

Are you not funking,
      to clear out,
             shake off
What you no longer need?
      Or is it just
Sheer greed!

Fears tend to be self-fulfilling: don't use them to put up barriers which place you out of reach of life's joys.

Don't let
Fears
        interfere
With your trust in life
                    right here:
        it will make
                    the dreaded
Come near
        and nearer
Until it has no choice
            but to appear unfurled
In this,
        out daylight world.

Life
Is for living out,
Not cautiously withdrawing
        behind the ramparts of one's fear
That yesterday's disasters
                    might reoccur.

    Past tragedies
Will only reappear
            if dread is not restrained
        from steering us
Clear of the better times
                    existence
Has learned to engineer
                since yesteryear.

It doesn't help to blame life for the choices that you have made. Examine these more closely – there are lessons to be learnt – and then move on to what is waiting for you just around the corner.

I've seen a lot –

and I am seeing more –
clearly,
Those ghastly things

we're laying at the door
of good old Life

turn out to be
Not true at all –   sheer blasphemy!

It took me all my years to see
That every bit of fear,

crippling anxiety
Was groundless,

had no reality
But that
which we
Had strenuously mocked up
Into a miraged actuality-construct.
And it's those phantom fears
Which steer us into useless strife
Making a cock-up

of the tasty brew of life.

Yes,
I've seen a lot,

have done a lot,
though there is more

still left undone,
But I have had my run –
and I suspect
It's nothing like

what's waiting
Just outside that door...

Go peacefully about your daily business: thus you lessen the negative impact of life's 'slings and arrows'.

Of late
        I've come into
A lot of peace...
                and even
When I ease
          or rather
     stir myself
             a little out of it,
It seems
        the nitty-gritty grind
       has lost its sting -
          the traffic's roar
       no more offends my ears –
          almost
       appears to sing!

And yet
        I then
Don't miss a thing!

Which makes me wonder
       what all our anxious efforting
Is for...!

An illness can convey an important message to the sufferer – the mistake lies in trying to cover it up!

A healing
          must not stop the illness
    from revealing
The misuse
         of a part of life in us
We have been foolishly concealing.

All that we are
          and have on board
Is needed on our voyage
    can only at our peril
Be ignored.

Trying to control the future in every detail only imposes a stranglehold on it and makes your progress that much harder.

The future
Will come –
        and have its way!
But how it will present itself,
    appear
        on our little bio-sphere,
The focus of our eyes and ears,
        our hopes and fears
Will build into a scene,
        a plot
In which we have a part to play.

And only then
        can we put up with –
    bear the harsher things
Without despair!

Humanity has acquired vast experience – much of it contributed by those who are 'different' from you! Integrating these differences will add much to your growth process.

The Era of Exploring
    what each is
                on its own
    is clearly
At an end:
    now we must learn
To blend our different-nesses once again!

If we by now
             have not begun to see
Our meaning,
          value lies
But in Community of everything
            of all there is,
The pains of differentiating,
          separating out,
                dissecting,
Will have been in vain,
    and we'll have missed
The whole point of life's exercise.

If you learn to listen to the higher powers, they in turn will have no need to grab your attention and will guide you more gently and without drama!

You,
      our helpers!
We *do* have ears
To listen!
      there is no longer any need
      to steer us
By disasters,
            by defeat,
                  the pain
            of sheer frustration:
      the fear of further humiliation
Does not improve our steering –
                  indeed
      an accident you engineered
May keep us off the road for good –
                  forever!
      Which makes your guidance
Seem none too clever...

      Perhaps
The Ultimate could well do worse
      than run
Urgent refresher-courses
      for its assistants on this earth...

Dreams are the driving seat of creativity and inspiration and our defence against uncertainty and confusion.

Our dreams
Are torches that we light
To stave off the infinite
in the night
of our vast loneliness,
In the heavy fog
of our bewilderment,
In the searching twilight
of our deeds,
or in memory
Of a love
that is no more...

Dreams
Are lit windows
in the distance.

Love is the most powerful life force!
Do not seek to understand it, or
divert it – just let it flow!

Now
Only love will do.

And though
    the young
           revel in dreams of love,
    the old
        think back on it,
    the cold ones
          bait their traps,
    the cruel
         cut with love,
    the maudlin
          splutter it,
    the wise
         persist in counselling love,
Still no one knows it,
    none can tell me
          what
            – and where –
    Love is...

    Yet
Only love will do now,
Only love
      will do
    for *me*.

If where you are now upsets you, remember you planned to be here and had good reasons for it once!

Don't sigh –
                don't cry!
        Whatever
                    I turn out to be today,
It's I
Who made me go that way!

            And what is more,
I must have known
                        why and what for...

Slow down,
                calm down:
        I am –
                have always been
A clown
            ...and clowns
Don't frown!

You live in both your inner and your outer worlds – make sure that they are in balance and each features in who you are.

The *inner* world
Is always blooming –
It is the *real* world
                              before our open eyes
          where we inaugurated
Gloom and doom –
                         while life
Is constant flowering,
                         cannot be otherwise!
          But we alas
Do have the power
To turn it down
                         until its veins
Seem to silt up –
                    days
Wilt into a desertscape,
          the so distressing mess
Of this
          our so-called 'real'
Phantom wilderness!

          The inner world
Is not just resting-place
   from struggling through the 'real' day:
It is our native land,
                         our homeground's soil
          and whereabouts
                         in the infinity
          of all that's come to be
Life's down-to-earth reality.

Let's live our 'inner' world
For all it's worth!

Only by living life to the fullest and interacting to the best of your ability do you fulfil the divine plan.

The laws of life
                    are written
In the things we meet;
And there's nowhere else
        where we can read,
                            see,
                                touch
The features of our God
        but in the splendour of a tree,
        the blossoms blaze,
        the mellow meadows:
        in the living earth under our feet –
As in another's nearness,
                            smile –
        that sunshine on my face
                            and soul.

Only in living
            do I see my God
Complete
            and whole.

There is no room for complacency!
Keep going or you will simply stop
growing.

                   Contrive
To keep arriving –
                               for
            having got there
Is the end
               to dreaming on:
            no dream –
                        no more creating –
            no more creating –
                              no taking in :
            no give-and-take relating
And without that
You cease to be.

See
        that your striving
                              does not end
            upon arriving.

            On getting there
Note your progress
And press on:
                     attaining
Must not bend the endless quest
            Back
 Into ending
               our Eternal gaining!

Celebrate the joys of life. The light which you then cast will steadily grow and touch all those around you!

Let's celebrate
The joy of life
        each in himself,
                in every cell
                of all of us,
Until your glow
           of steadily expanding light
   ignites
And boosts it all around!

And then
          you will have found
The high-ground of your destiny.
     The same as that
 For which the whole of Earth is bound:
The blaze of revelling Love of Life
     must now
 No longer be hemmed in,
               confined
By brooding-moping night!

   Come,
Let us climb at last out of the pit
And celebrate *all* joy:
The Universe is standing by
     waiting for us
To do our bit.

It is up to you to decide what you choose to get out of life! It is no use blaming fate or destiny for your own choices.

There always is
    a way
 Back into life –
        at any time!

    The living vine
Is ever climbing
To yield the wine sublime
    to quench our thirst
For more of life –
Unless we turn the tumbler upside down
    and stop the press
Distilling the elixir divine:
    or
Teeter at the brink
        if one's too glum
          or dumb –
    to know
How much one likes the blissful drink!

    The choice
Is never fate's
      nor destiny's alone
But yours and mine.

Take life at a measured pace in order to explore it to the full. Your hopes and desires will then fall into place...

I suppose
It's no skin off this Oldie's nose
    to propose
That going slow
Is better than rushing –
    to take things easy
Is always worth one's while!

    I know
I'm not exactly gushing
With the urging energy of youth
    but then
My longings,
        ardent hopes
    are now as hard to quell
As ever:
      young or old,
           dumb or clever,
All hopes and longings
        are quite apart
From any living,
      pulsing heart.
    And that is
Just as well…

Learn to trust your instincts. They tell you all you need to know...

The first
Whispers
       of the day
Say all there is to say
   and later
Will be said
       more loudly
For the but vaguely listening ears.

Alas,
More loudly said,
   truth's potent essence
Disappears...

The past has had its day and the future is undecided. Live in the present moment, and the future can then take shape...

             I had my spell
In hell:
             I say farewell
To anything but fun,
                          delight.

I shall rejoice
                 shall revel
In every little pleasure
                 I can find – or borrow –
And fan it to full heat
        to have it climb into
                              and stay
Right at the zenith of my sky,
        making my sunny firmament
Complete:
             I might be blind to life
Tomorrow!

        O, I shall warble
Every song
             that's in my throat to sing –
        bring voice
To all and everything
Wants to be said
                     and heard:
        tomorrow
I might be deaf
             or dead!

        This
Is my choice.

It is all a question of perspective. Although we are part of the self-same reality, allow for the delicate interplay of differences and viewpoints – your life will be the richer for it...

I thought
       I see you
As you are,
    but then
To a crow
       we far below
Will be all head and arms –
To a frog
All feet
      and legs on the go…

To think
      I thought
I knew
What is good for you!
    Charming
       if not alarming!
Then too –
     although we both,
         we all
    are part of one reality,
The way you are
Is not the only way to be:
Just look at me!

Why be in such a headlong rush that you run down your physical health? You cannot make the best choice if you overlook the clues that life offers...

Rushing,
        pushing
Makes you overlook the clues
How to go –
        which route to choose –
        which turning best to take.
   And you ignore
The traffic lights:
You have to slam the brakes on hard –
Until it not just shakes your car
But your own vital parts to bits.

Dim-wits we are...

Others see qualities and possibilities in you which you may have excluded for yourself. Acknowledge that these exist and you will grow into a larger reality.

     Do you
Really
Not want to have me dream of you?
     I certainly
              would want you to see
The dream of me
          rather than
My drab reality:

Our dreaming of each other
Will help us grow
           into much more
    than so far
We succeed to be.

Remember you are a powerful being. Take charge and LIVE life: don't just let it happen to you!

        It is
Far easier
        to place another
Into the clouds
                    above shared ground,
        than face
                    up to
How tall we are;
                    how sound,
                        how far along;
        how godly masterful
Each one of us
                    was made to be
To *guide* this life,
        not see it
Bossing us around!

Oh, what a farçe –
        what cruel,
                        tragic
    Travesty!

The intuitive 'child' within each of us is often wiser than the adult that we grow to be. If you are seeking an answer – look to the inner child...

I knew
So much more
When I was a child,
        and then
I was wild with joy...
        but luckily
That early curly me
Lives on inside,
        alongside all,
The bald-pate clown
I've grown
                – or shrunk –
To be.

Every barrier, every separation, each alienation that we bring into our lives is ultimately an illusion.

We do build lonelinesses
                                    – this I know –
         as we go along:
         cruel
Illusion
Of being separate,
                         out on one's own
        when we all live
Inside each other
        as much
As in our self –
        never
Alone...

Each individual choice and direction interweaves to create our joint reality. Take responsibility for your creation...

When all is said and done,
You
 can only do to me
What I *let* you do:
 I must admit
It's up to me
  to see to it
That it is fun
  at least for me –
If not for you
  and everyone!

Which path you take,
 in that
The future is at stake
Not just for you or me:
Your choice and mine
 combine
To form Man's destiny.

To play an effective part within this three-dimensional world, it is essential to stay grounded in order to keep on track.

No more
Than anchored
        in reality we are
So that we don't get blown away,
           off course
By any random craft,
        some hiccup
    in the cosmic scheme –
Nor to be swept back
        to what has been:
But stay on track –
A working part
Within the present scene.

If you are negative with others you slow down their progress as well as your own.

Do not sow doubt,
                        not even
For the sake of truth:
        when someone's
Being glad to be alive,
        is all at stake,
                        what does it matter
What door the joy-infusion takes
                        to enter through –
        what difference does it make
To you?!

Magic – the enchantment of the unexpected can lift you above the daily grind of life! It brings renewal as well as hope...

     Without enchantment
Nothing new is born –
     without enchantment
Nothing lasts:
           the worn-out,
                torn
Is not regrown!

     Oh,
          unenchanted,
     nothing
Can outlive the past!

You are experiencing a temporary setback. Everything is on course and you will see the benefits of this soon...

Snow in mid-April?
Too late
          for a joke –
Too late for fooling anyone:

Spring has begun;
Winter
          has had its day,
          and if it powders
Budding trees
With clouds of Christmas stillness,
No one is taken in:

          Spring shakes it off
With a summer's grin,
For
          – come what may –
Summer is drawing near
          will soon be here!
Summer
          is
On his way!

The interaction between your innermost self and the physical world is complementary. Strive to stay in balance regarding where you put your energy.

We need to know
There is a world
      outside our windows
  as well as one
From which we're looking out at it,
  for,
While the outside world
     gives us the food we need
The inside world does the digesting
To feed the living essences of us –
Those seabirds
     hovering
Above both worlds
     and maybe
Many more
    that we don't know
As universes go...

If you are stuck in a rut, consider: is it merely habit that keeps you where you are?

Why don't we want
To be aware of –
              bear in mind –
       what we behind it all
Well know?

       Why do we not forgo
What clearly does not work,
                     will always fail
       and keep on stepping
Into the same old traps
       to get stuck
              in the same old muck!
As if discomfort,
                suffering and pain
Were really fun
                for everyone,
Joy but a stain on life
                and happiness a bane!

       Surely
We have not been created
To be so hopelessly inane,
                     downright insane!

Do not narrow down your choices so that you exclude all that contributes to growth. Trust life and trust your own capacity to deal with it...

>   Mine
> Is a solitary song
>   – oh so alone –
> Trying to say
>   as simply as one can
> What has been known to Man
>   for as long
> As he has swept it out of sight:
>   as if we would see better
> Without light!
>
> Because more brightness
> Might stun the eyes
> And startle,
>   wake
>   and overheat
> The dozy heart?
>
> Better an aching,
>   quaking heart,
>   stunned eyes
> Than none at all to keep us
> From sliding,
>   falling back
> Into the dreary scene
> The vastly wanting past has been –
>   painful enough
> To stunt one's love of life
>
>   Now
> I'd rather buy the future
>   sight unseen!

Don't let the ebb and flow of life cause you to switch course in midstream without asking yourself what your true goals are...

I walk towards you
Before dawn,
    but once you raise
The curtain of the day,
I walk the other way –
Back to the things
That need your light.

    And though
I only follow but your flow
I also head for Night.

    To rest perhaps?
As well as
    for another dawn –
As many dawns as I can find,
      for without you
I am forlorn,
    my days
Still-born and blind.

Once you still the restlessness within yourself, you can see the overall plan emerging triumphant and complete – and your own role within it!

Although
The seagull of my soul
Is not a docile bird,
    now
That the shrieks of hungry beaks
    are no more heard,
        my eyes
Can hear the radiance of the sun,
The ear
    can see the music of the wind,
        and I can sense
The interweaving
    of the pleasing
        with the paining.
The blending
        of ending
    and beginning
Fusing
The ceasing of what had begun
With the emerging rebirth
    of the ceased,
        released at last
From dying's shocking mock finality!

Whether you know it or not, you are on a journey, and all journeys must end eventually...

'Don't try to rush Me'
                        says the Lord –
    'You know
You are on board My ship –
    I cannot have it skip
Instead of sail along
                    the sea
That's also Me!

Calm down:
            all lives
Arrive eventually.'

THE END

The Writer's Epilogue

If you are anything like me,
    These poems ought to be
Some help
    In making your own way
                 from day to day.

I know
    that I for one
    could well have done
With some more help
          than I received,
    and if I'm not deceived,
Is that not just as true of you?

But should you have no need
    of any line
         of mine,
You must be doing fine!
    And I –
         with you –
Shall feel indeed relieved.

Contents and Index of first lines